INTRODUCTION

Earthquakes strike with devastating force and often without warning. Approximately 41 US states are at risk of moderate to severe earthquakes, and amazingly, these states are located in every region of the country.

An earthquake is an effect from shifting tectonic plates below the Earth's crust. The sudden and violent shaking can collapse buildings and bridges and may trigger surface events like landslides, floods, avalanches, fires and huge, destructive ocean waves, called Tsunami.

When an earthquake occurs in a heavily populated area, damages can include loss of life and property. Ground movement during an earthquake is rarely the direct cause of loss of life. More often, it is the resulting damage to structures and roadways that have the most devastating impact.

Scientists have proved that earthquakes will occur in areas that have previously had them, so one important step in learning about your earthquake risk is to learn about the history – no matter how old – of prior earthquakes in your area.

Preparation is Key

1. Know the Dangers

Earthquakes usually occur in predictable patterns around the country. If you are new to the area or just developing your survival awareness, learn about the earthquake potential in your area. Contact your state emergency management office or local American Red Cross to learn more.

2. Learn Basic Survival Skills

Earthquakes have predictable effects: typically buildings and roadways are damaged; power is knocked out, which, in turn, causes water and heating/cooling systems to fail. As a result, people can be without drinkable water, light, heat or air conditioning for days. The lack of post-disaster survival know-how creates terrible suffering and costs hundreds of lives each year.

3. Don't Panic

Staying calm is the most important thing you can do when an earthquake strikes. Excitement and alarm are natural emotions, but you must be able to manage them in order to make good decisions. Compose yourself and others and take charge of the situation.

4. Have an Action Plan

Personal safety, shelter and security are always your highest priority. Your first concern is to avoid injuries and stay safe until conditions return to normal.

- Determine the safest place to endure an earthquake at home and away.
- Prepare personal survival kits for every individual in your household, including pets.
- Have a plan to connect with friends and family during and after the earthquake so you can ensure everyone stays safe.

Made in the USA

Waterford Press produces reference guides that introduce novices to nature, science, travel and languages. Product information is featured on the website: **www.waterfordpress.com**

Text and illustrations © 2015, 2019 by Waterford Press Inc. All rights reserved. Cover images © iStock Photo. Map copyright © USGS 2015.

To order, call 800-434-2555. For permissions, or to share comments, e-mail editor@waterfordpress.com. For information on custom-published products, call 800-434-2555 or e-mail info@waterfordpress.com.

ISBN 978-1-58355-858-4 $7.95 U.S.
50795
9 781583 558584
UPC 8 84682 01160 4
10 9 8 7 6 5 4 3 2 1 909205

EARTHQUAKE SURVIVAL – PREPARE FOR & SURVIVE AN EARTHQUAKE

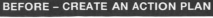

A DISASTER SURVIVAL GUIDE

EARTHQUAKE SURVIVAL

PREPARE FOR & SURVIVE AN EARTHQUAKE

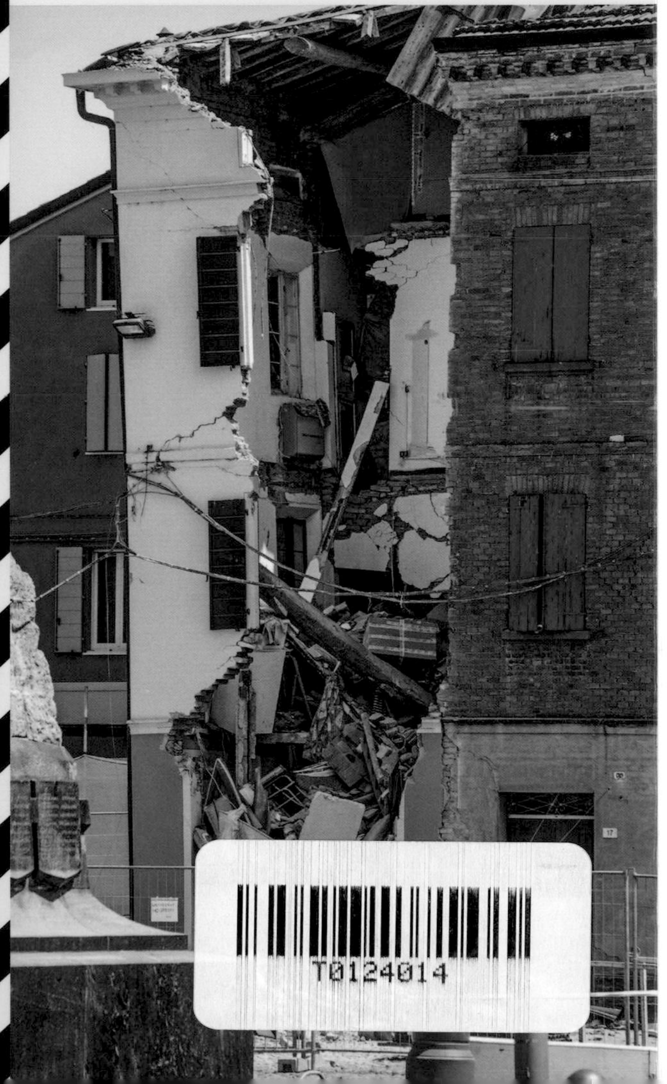

T0124014

BEFORE – HOW TO PREPARE

National Seismic Hazard Map

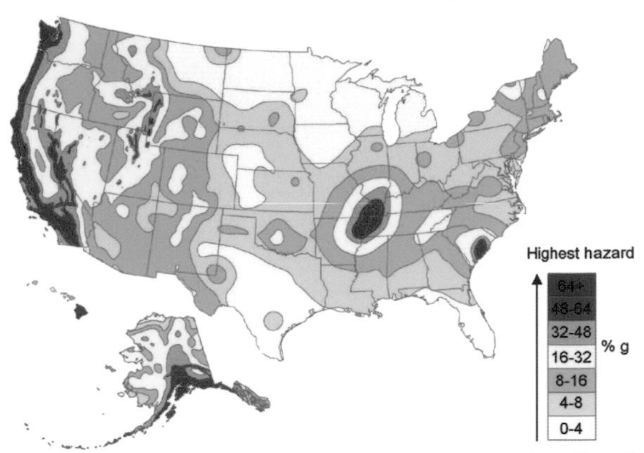
Highest hazard
64+
48-64
32-48
16-32
8-16
4-8
0-4
% g
Lowest hazard

Prepare Your Home to Survive an Earthquake

Although there are no guarantees of safety during an earthquake, identifying potential hazards ahead of time and advance planning can save lives and significantly reduce injuries and property damage.

While it is impossible to predict an earthquake, people in earthquake-prone areas can prepare by following a few simple guidelines:

- Bolt tall furniture such as bookshelves, clocks, cabinets and other top-heavy items to the wall, making sure you connect them securely to wall studs.
- Place large or heavy objects, breakable items, pesticides and flammable products on lower shelves of latched cabinets.
- Fasten heavy items such as pictures and mirrors securely to walls and away from beds, couches and anywhere people sit.
- Brace overhead light fixtures.
- Secure your water heater, refrigerator, furnace and gas appliances by strapping them to the wall studs and bolting them to the floor.
- Secure appliances and equipment such as televisions and computers so they will not fall during an earthquake.
- Secure (chain down) external propane bottles to prevent damage and/or theft.
- Have professionals install flexible fittings for gas and water lines to help avoid breaks.
- Check with local authorities about building standards and structural requirements pertaining to your home. Ask about home improvements to strengthen decks, sliding doors, carports and other attached or detached elements that can be dislodged or damaged during an earthquake.

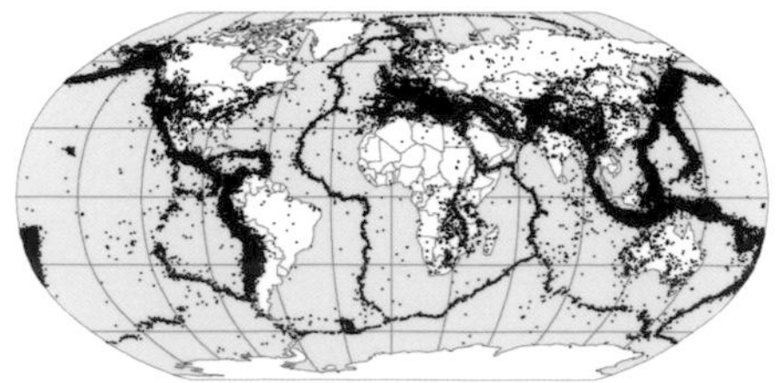

Earthquake Events Worldwide 1963-1999

BEFORE – WHAT TO EXPECT

System Failures

Power Failure

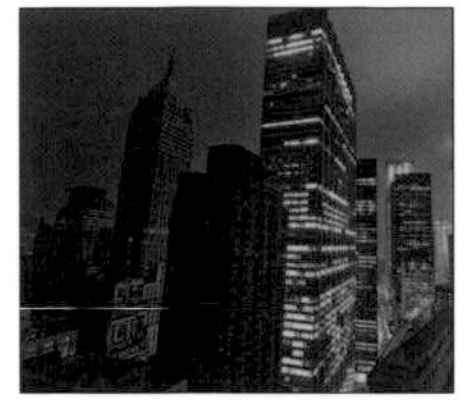

Electricity cut off. Downed power lines present risk of electrocution, especially if the lines are downed in water. They may also hinder your ability to leave the area. It may take days or weeks for power to return.

Water Failure

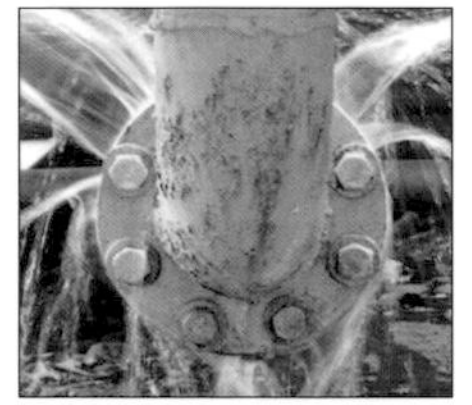

Water lines become damaged, water pressure fails and running water ceases. Toilets become unusable. If water lines are damaged, the water supply becomes contaminated. When water pressure returns, the water is undrinkable.

Gas Failure

Gas lines rupture and gas system fails. If gas lines are damaged, leaks present risk of poisoning, explosions and fires. Once shut off, only gas companies can restore service, which may take weeks.

Personal Risks

Injury

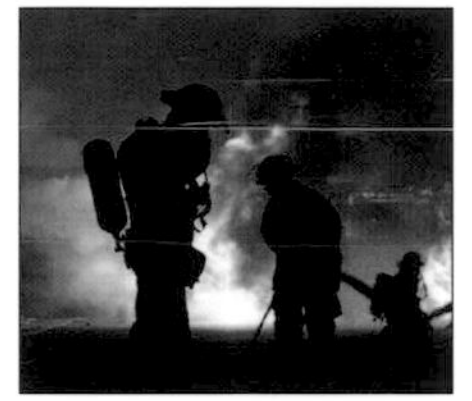

Falling objects can cause deep cuts, broken bones and potentially entrap people. Trauma of events can induce heart attack.

Looting/Theft

People who are unprepared may panic and steal possessions from stores, households and individuals to survive. Have some form of defense – pepper spray or a weapon – to protect you and your family from harm.

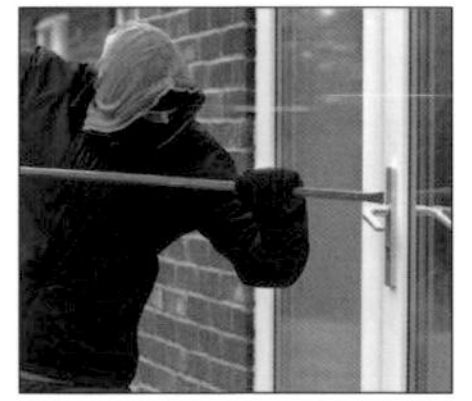

Isolation/Restricted Movement

Earthquakes commonly damage roads and bridges, which strand people where they are at the time of the event. Structural damage to homes will either trap people inside or prevent access to their homes afterward.

Earthquake Alerts

There are very few instances when emergency authorities can alert people to earthquake potential. Some obvious alerts include the occurrence of an earthquake elsewhere – a quake in Asia, for instance, can potentially trigger the after effects as far away as the Pacific coast of the USA.

Scan for more info

National Weather Service

Earthquakes often include multiple shaking events – either after-shocks, which are smaller shakes that follow the main event or, on the other hand, sometimes "small rumbles" that we experience are preliminary events or "foreshocks" that will be followed by a larger shock.

In all cases, the minute an earthquake is reported or experienced, you are best advised to treat it as a preliminary event, likely to be followed by more. That way, you will take the necessary actions to protect your family and property.

BEFORE – CREATE AN ACTION PLAN

1. Determine the Safest Place to Endure the Event

Establish safe places in every location where you or your family can take shelter during the event, including schools, libraries, day care – both inside and outside of your home. The safest place to survive an earthquake is usually the most structurally sound part of a building. In a house, choose a closet, bathroom or windowless, interior hallway on the lowest floor. Make sure to keep this area uncluttered. Consider having the area reinforced to ensure it is strong enough to withstand an earthquake. In high rise buildings, the safest area is typically near the elevator shafts and emergency exits.

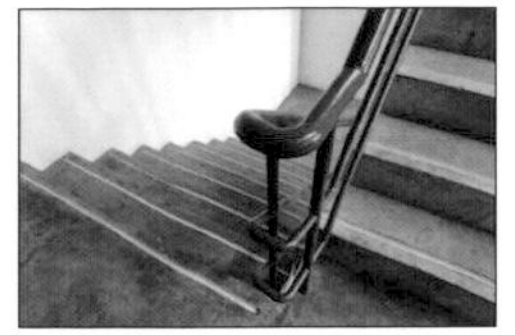

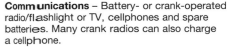

2. Know Your Local Support Network & Evacuation Routes

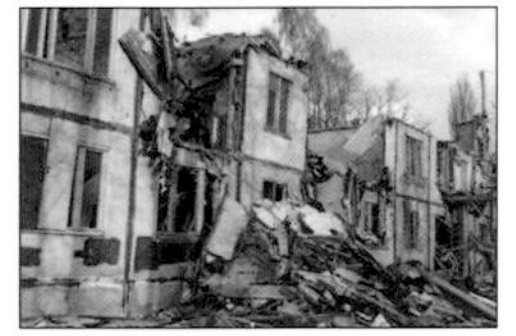

When an earthquake strikes, survival can depend on a few basic elements. Access to clean water, shelter, warmth/cool and sanitation can be a matter of life or death in the days and weeks after the event.

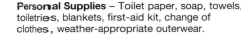

- Where are public shelters and evacuation routes, should you be required to move from your home before or after the earthquake? Determine where you would go and how you would get there if you needed to evacuate.
- If you have special needs such as elderly, disabled or chronically ill members in your family, what will they need and where will they go in case of disaster? Make similar arrangements for your pets.
- Know the disaster plans in places you routinely spend time such as your workplace, your children's daycare or schools.

3. Make a Family Action Plan

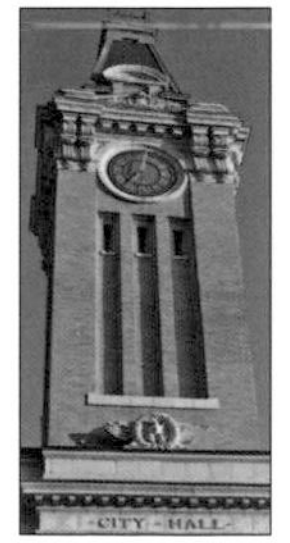

- Create a card of key contacts for each family member. Have a designated contact out of the immediate area. While local phone systems may be overloaded, you can often get through to an out-of-area contact.
- Pick two places for your family to reunite after the earthquake if you are apart when it strikes. One location can be your home and the other a landmark that is easy to access.
- Let relatives or friends know the location of your safe room/area so they will know where to find you if you are trapped and/or injured.

4. Practice Earthquake Response

Practice retreating to safe places with your family members. When an earthquake strikes, the family response should be immediate and automatic. Rehearse steps to get to your safe places from various locations.

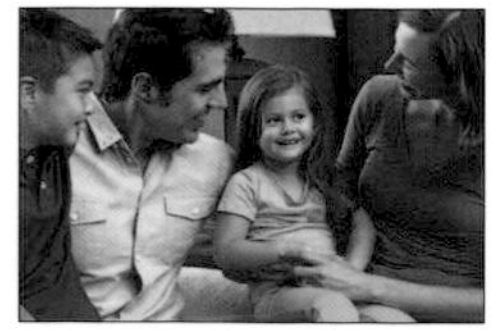

Practice "drop, cover and hold-on" with all family members. There will be no time to think – you and your family need an immediate, instinctive reaction that comes from having planned and rehearsed prior to the event. Learn emergency first aid and CPR to be able to help yourself and others if needed.

BEFORE – PREPARE SURVIVAL KITS

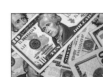

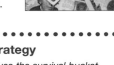

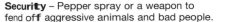

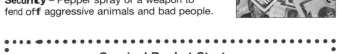

5. Prepare a Personal Survival Kit for Each Individual

Each kit should sustain an individual for three days. Put the following in a waterproof plastic container and place in an easily accessible location. Have a similar mini-kit in each vehicle.

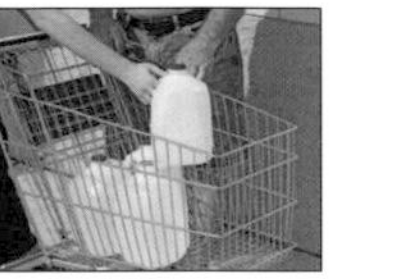

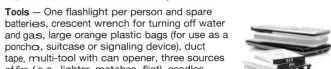

Water & Food – Three gallons of drinking water and water purification tablets. Food is not essential since you can live for weeks without eating. If you choose to include foods, they should be low in salt and high in calories and require no refrigeration or preparation (e.g., peanut butter, canned or dry food items). Replace water and food in kit every six months.

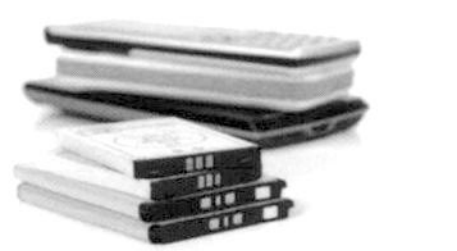

Tools – One flashlight per person and spare batteries, crescent wrench for turning off water and gas, large orange plastic bags (for use as a poncho, suitcase or signaling device), duct tape, multi-tool with can opener, three sources of fire (e.g., lighter, matches, flint), candles, pens, paper, 50 ft. of rope and a signal whistle.

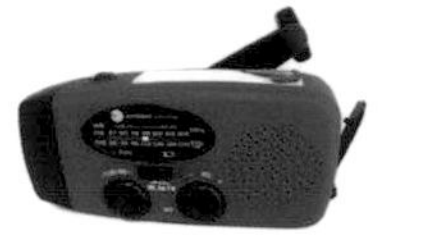

Communications – Battery- or crank-operated radio/flashlight or TV, cellphones and spare batteries. Many crank radios can also charge a cellphone.

Personal Supplies – Toilet paper, soap, towels, toiletries, blankets, first-aid kit, change of clothes, weather-appropriate outerwear.

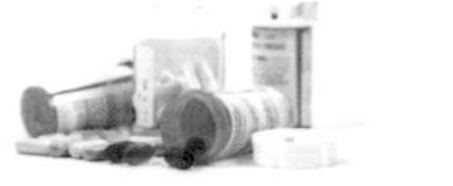

Special Needs Items – Baby formula, diapers, **medications and specialized medical equipment**, glasses, pet food, etc.

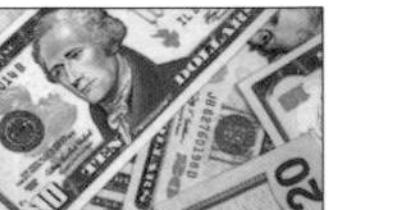

Paperwork – Identification (carry with you at all times). Contact info for family, friends and emergency services, cash (small bills) and credit cards, copies of insurance papers, mortgage, bank accounts, proof of occupancy (utility bill). Keep paperwork in a separate waterproof container.

Security – Pepper spray or a weapon to fend off aggressive animals and bad people.

Survival Bucket Strategy

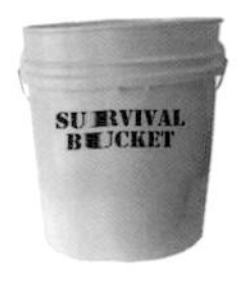
SURVIVAL
BUCKET

A simple way to prepare for disasters is to use the survival bucket strategy. Simply put, every member of a household – including pets – should have a sturdy five gallon bucket with a lid that contains enough supplies for them to survive 3 DAYS without water or power. Fill it with your survival gear (excluding phones, medications and paperwork), seal it, label it and store it where it is easy to find. Add the missing items at the last minute. A bucket is the ideal storage device because it is waterproof and also has many additional uses including stool/table, flotation device, wash basin, solar still, noisemaker for signal, water heater, bailing tool, toilet and shovel.

Scan this code to purchase survival bucket supplies online.

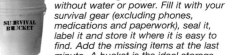

IF YOU ARE INDOORS

Drop, Cover and Hold On. Minimize your movements to a few steps to a nearby safe place and if you are indoors, stay there until the shaking has stopped and you are sure exiting is safe.

DROP to the ground;

take **COVER** by getting under a sturdy table or other piece of furniture; and

HOLD ON until the shaking stops.

If there isn't a table or desk near you, cover your face and head with your arms and crouch in an inside corner of the building.

• Stay away from glass, windows, outside doors and walls, and anything that could fall, such as lighting fixtures or bookcases. In high-rise buildings, expect fire alarms and sprinklers to be triggered by an earthquake.

• If you are in bed when the earthquake strikes, stay there unless you are under a heavy lighting fixture or object that may fall. Protect your head with a pillow or covers.

• Do not use a doorway unless you know it is a strongly supported, load-bearing doorway and it is close to you. Many inside doorways are lightly constructed and do not offer protection.

• Stay inside until the shaking stops and it is safe to go outside. Do not exit a building during the shaking. Research has shown that most injuries occur when people inside buildings attempt to move to a different location inside the building or try to leave.

IF YOU ARE OUTDOORS

• Stay outside. Avoid running since you may be thrown about or fall into a fissure.

• Move away from buildings, streetlights, power lines and trees. Stay out of tunnels that may collapse.

• Once in the open, stay there until the shaking stops. The greatest danger exists directly outside buildings.

IF YOU ARE IN A VEHICLE

• Stop as quickly as safety permits and stay in the vehicle; it will protect you from falling objects. Avoid stopping near or under buildings, trees, overpasses, and utility wires. Crouch down on the floor and wait for tremors to pass.

• Proceed cautiously once the earthquake has stopped. Avoid roads, bridges, or ramps that might have been damaged by the earthquake.

DROP

COVER

HOLD ON

If no protection is available, protect your head with your arms and crouch.

> Most earthquake-related casualties result from collapsing walls, flying glass, and falling objects.

EXPECT AFTERSHOCKS, TSUNAMIS, LANDSLIDES

Secondary shockwaves are usually less violent than the main quake but can be strong enough to do additional damage to weakened structures. They can occur in the first hours, days, weeks, or even months after the quake.

If you live in coastal areas, giant seismic sea waves may occur following an earthquake. When local authorities issue a tsunami warning, assume that a series of dangerous waves is on the way. Stay away from the beach. If you are in a mountainous area, watch for landslides, falling rocks and other debris that may have been loosened by the earthquake.

Once you are certain the earthquake has passed, do a quick evaluation of the condition of your shelter/home and the people in it.

1. Is Your Location Still Safe and Secure?

If you see something that is unsafe, take your survival kit and get everyone out of the building immediately. An aftershock could create further instability and more potential for injury.

• Look for damage and fires in your immediate surroundings. **Fire is the most common hazard after an earthquake.** Extinguish small fires if you are able.

• If you smell gas, hear a hissing or blowing noise, immediately leave the building. If you can, turn off the gas at the outside main valve and call the gas company or notify emergency personnel of the damage.

• If you see frayed wiring or sparks, or if there is an odor of something burning, leave the building unless you are able to shut off the electrical system at the main circuit breaker.

• If your location is not safe and secure and has become damaged, go to a designated public shelter. **Text SHELTER + your ZIP code to 4FEMA** to find the nearest shelter in your area.

• **If you are trapped**, do not light a match. Create a signal to draw attention to your location. Tap on a pipe or wall so rescuers can locate you. Use a whistle if one is available. Shout only as a last resort. Shouting can cause you to inhale dangerous amounts of dust.

• If electric power goes out, unplug or shut off all of your large appliances (fridges, televisions, etc.) so that when electricity is restored, appliances are not damaged by the surge.

Scan for more info

FEMA

2. Is Anyone Injured or Trapped?

Help injured or trapped persons. Check on neighbors who may require special assistance with infants, the elderly and people with accessibility and medical/functional needs.

• Assess and treat any minor injuries as you are qualified and able to do so. Stop a bleeding injury by applying direct pressure to the wound. When bleeding stops, apply a dry sterile dressing. Have any serious injuries evaluated by a physician as soon as possible.

• Do not attempt to move seriously injured people unless they are in immediate danger of further injury. Get medical assistance immediately. If someone has stopped breathing, begin CPR.

---

3. Making Contact With Others

Contact family members and friends to ensure they do not need assistance. If you or a member of your family become separated or goes missing, DO NOT CALL THE POLICE; they will be overwhelmed with other demands. Instead, contact the American Red Cross at 1-800-RED-CROSS/1-800-733-2767.

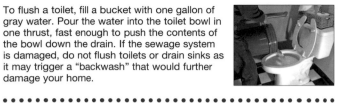

Scan for more info

Red Cross

4. Moving Around After an Earthquake

When the shaking stops, look around to make sure it is safe to move before exiting a building. In high-rise buildings, follow the emergency exit stairs to evacuate. Never use an elevator.

As you prepare to move, remember that personal safety is your highest priority. Moving can expose you to potential injuries and create further problems if you are not careful. Protect yourself from further injury by putting on appropriate clothes – shirts, long pants, boots and gloves if they are available. Watch for falling objects. Look for and extinguish small fires.

General Safety Considerations

• Continue to monitor your cellphone, radio or television for emergency information. Stay alert for subsequent events even after the earthquake has ended.

• If you are away from home, do not return until authorities say it is safe to do so.

• Be careful when moving through structures that have been damaged.

• Check for leaking gas and water and electrical problems. If you suspect any damage to your home, shut off all electrical power, natural gas and propane tanks to avoid fire, electrocution or explosions. Use battery-powered lanterns or headlamps rather than gas-powered lamps or candles for light sources when the power is out.

• Do not go near downed power lines or objects in contact with downed lines. If water is in the vicinity of downed lines, the whole area may be electrified. Report electrical hazards to the police and the affected utility company.

• Open cabinets cautiously. Beware of objects that can fall off shelves.

• Clean up spilled medicines, drugs, flammable liquids and other potentially hazardous materials that could become a fire hazard.

• Do not use tap water unless you are certain it is safe; cracks in pipes can cause inadvertent flooding and risk of contamination.

• Check your heating ducts for blockages; blocked systems can cause a buildup of carbon monoxide. If you have any doubts, have an expert inspect the system before turning on furnaces or air conditioners.

• For insurance purposes, take pictures of any damages.

UNSEEN HAZARDS

• Carbon monoxide
• Contaminated water
• Electrocution
• Falling objects

Survival Priorities

Statistically speaking, the most likely causes of death during a disaster are becoming too cold (hypothermia) or too hot (hyperthermia). Depending on where you live – Anchorage vs. Phoenix – your survival strategy and the contents of your survival kit should be adapted to suit your environment.

Shelter

Protection from the elements will allow you to preserve strength and restore energy. If your safe area becomes compromised during the storm, either repair the damages or move to another shelter.

In Cold Weather

1. Insulate an area suitable for the number of people in your group. Close large openings with duct tape and tarps, plastic, cardboard or blankets, depending on what is available to you. **BE CAREFUL** to leave adequate airflow or you will suffocate!

2. Protect yourself from loss of body warmth by adding layers of dry materials – cardboard, rugs, blankets, cushions, clothing or mattresses – between you and the floor or earth.

3. Stay as dry as possible.

In Warm Weather

1. Stay as hydrated as possible; limit exertion.

2. Protect yourself from the elements; stay out of the sun and wind, which deplete hydration.

3. Stay on the lowest floor of your house, where it is coolest. If outdoors, seek the safest source of shade and build your shelter around/under that. If there is ample fresh water available, wet your clothes to increase cooling.

Water

You can only survive 3 days without water, and even less in hot, arid surroundings. Carefully ration the fresh water you have for drinking only (one gallon per person per day under normal conditions). Never waste water; after use for cooking and bathing, it can be used as gray water for other purposes.

Drinking Water

Can be obtained from several sources. In addition to the water stored in tub(s) and sinks, sources of fresh water inside a building include:

Water pipes – Once you shut off the water to a building, the water pipes remain full of water. Turn off your hot water heater and water treatment system and drain the water from the pipes via taps into food-quality containers.

Hot water heater – The hot water heater in most homes contains 20-30 gallons of water. Simply drain from the faucet at the bottom.

Toilet tanks – Each holds 2-4 gallons. Purify before drinking.

Hot water heater

Gray Water

Use gray water from streams, ponds, puddles and snowmelt for uses other than drinking. Most gray water can be purified for drinking if needed.

To flush a toilet, fill a bucket with one gallon of gray water. Pour the water into the toilet bowl in one thrust, fast enough to push the contents of the bowl down the drain. If the sewage system is damaged, do not flush toilets or drain sinks as it may trigger a "backwash" that would further damage your home.

How to Purify Water

If the water system fails, NEVER drink tap water unless you are certain it is not contaminated. To be safe, water should always be purified before drinking.

Three simple ways to purify water are:

1. Bring water to a rolling boil for 10 minutes;

2. Treat with purification tablets, iodine (12 drops per gallon) or bleach (1/2 tablespoon per gallon);

3. Use a water pump or gravity-fed purifier to strain bacteria from the water.

Fire

With fire/heat you can purify water, control your core temperature, cook or preserve food and signal for rescue.

• Your survival kit should have at least three types of fire starter.

• Your barbecue, camping stove or gas lanterns are a potential source of heat that can be used to heat and purify water, warm foods and cook foods. Never use indoors; carbon monoxide released from these burning gases will kill you.

• Portable generators can provide temporary power to key sources like the refrigerator and heating/cooling system. Ensure you have enough gas to keep it running sporadically for several days.

The Silent Killer

Never use generators, grills, camp stoves or other gasoline, propane, natural gas or charcoal-burning devices inside your home, garage or camper. Carbon monoxide (CO) – an odorless, colorless gas that is given off when these fuels are burned – can cause sudden illness and death if you breathe it. If you suspect CO poisoning and are feeling dizzy, light-headed or nauseated, get into fresh air and seek medical help immediately. Even burning candles in an airtight room can cause asphyxiation and death.

Locate the main shutoff valves to your home or building before you are faced with an emergency. **Listen carefully to news reports that will inform you when to turn off your utilities.**

Power

Shut off electricity to the house to avoid power surges that can cause fires. Locate the power breaker box. If you have circuit breakers, there is usually a double breaker at the top of the row of breakers marked 'Main'. Flip that one and it shuts the house power off. Otherwise, simply turn off each individual breaker. Disconnect electrical appliances.

Water

To turn off the water to the building, locate the main shut-off valve (usually under a metal plate near the street at the front of the building). Lift off the plate and use a crescent wrench to turn the valve clockwise about 1/4 of a turn to shut the water off. In many homes, a secondary shut-off valve is located in the garage or basement. If the building is on a well, find out where the shut-off valve is.

Crescent Wrench

Gas

Gas lines can rupture, causing gas flow to fail. Leaking gas presents risks of poisoning, explosions and fires. Locate your gas meter outside the building. The shutoff valve is attached to the pipe coming out of the ground. Use a crescent wrench to turn the valve clockwise about 1/4 of a turn to shut off the gas. **Once the gas is turned off, you need a professional to turn it back on, which could take weeks.**

Emergency Etiquette

• Cooperate fully with public safety officials. If asked to relocate, do so immediately. Failure to relocate when asked creates an unfair load on emergency response personnel to find or rescue you, instead of on the community-wide recovery operations that will help everyone get back home as quickly and safely as possible.

• Only use your telephone for urgent calls to avoid tying up the available airspace.

• Keep your children and animals under your direct control.

• Report failures in power, water and gas to local utilities.

• Respond to requests for volunteer assistance by police, fire fighters and relief organizations, but **do not go into damaged areas unless assistance has been requested.**

• If you are going to a community shelter, bring your emergency supplies. Your stay will be more comfortable if you have your own food, water, clothes, blankets/sleeping bags and some items (books, cards, etc.) with which to pass the time. Access to power sources will be limited, so take extra batteries for your communications devices.